POETRY FROM CRESCENT MOON

William Shakespeare: *The Sonnets*
edited, with an introduction by Mark Tuley

William Shakespeare: *Complete Poems*
edited and introduced by Mark Tuley

*Shakespeare: Love, Poetry and Magic in Shakespeare's Sonnets
and Plays*
by B.D. Barnacle

Elizabethan Sonnet Cycles
edited and introduced by Mark Tuley

Edmund Spenser: *Heavenly Love: Selected Poems*
selected and introduced by Teresa Page

Edmund Spenser: *Amoretti*
edited by Teresa Page

Robert Herrick: *Delight In Disorder: Selected Poems*
edited and introduced by M.K. Pace

Sir Thomas Wyatt: *Love For Love: Selected Poems*
selected and introduced by Louise Cooper

John Donne: *Air and Angels: Selected Poems*
selected and introduced by A.H. Ninham

D.H. Lawrence: *Being Alive: Selected Poems*
edited with an introduction by Margaret Elvy

D.H. Lawrence: Symbolic Landscapes
by Jane Foster

D.H. Lawrence: Infinite Sensual Violence
by M.K. Pace

Percy Bysshe Shelley: *Paradise of Golden Lights: Selected Poems*
selected and introduced by Charlotte Greene

Thomas Hardy: *Her Haunting Ground: Selected Poems*
edited, with an introduction by A.H. Ninham

Idea

I D E A

Michael Drayton

Edited by Mark Tuley

CRESCENT MOON

CRESCENT MOON PUBLISHING
P.O. Box 1312, Maidstone
Kent, ME14 5XU
Great Britain
ww.crmoon.com

First published 2013. Reprinted 2020.

Set in Bodoni Book 11 on 13pt.
Designed by Radiance Graphics.

British Library Cataloguing in Publication data

ISBN-13 9781861716835
ISBN-13 9781861717764

CONTENTS

Michael Drayton

Michael Drayton

London around 1600

Idea

TO THE READER OF THESE SONNETS

Into these loves who but for passion looks,
At this first sight here let him lay them by,
And seek elsewhere in turning other books,
Which better may his labour satisfy.
No far-fetched sigh shall ever wound my breast;
Love from mine eye a tear shall never wring;
Nor in 'Ah me's!' my whining sonnets drest,
A libertine fantasticly I sing.
My verse is the true image of my mind,
Ever in motion, still desiring change;
To choice of all variety inclined,
And in all humours sportively I range.
  My muse is rightly of the English strain,
  That cannot long one fashion entertain.

I

Like an adventurous sea-farer am I,
Who hath some long and dang'rous voyage been,
And called to tell of his discovery,
How far he sailed, what countries he had seen,
Proceeding from the port whence he put forth,
Shows by his compass how his course he steered,
When east, when west, when south, and when by north,
As how the pole to every place was reared,
What capes he doubled, of what continent,
The gulfs and straits that strangely he had past,
Where most becalmed, where with foul weather spent,
And on what rocks in peril to be cast:
 Thus in my love, time calls me to relate
 My tedious travels and oft-varying fate.

II

My heart was slain, and none but you and I;
Who should I think the murder should commit?
Since but yourself there was no creature by
But only I, guiltless of murdering it.
It slew itself; the verdict on the view
Do quit the dead, and me not accessary.
Well, well, I fear it will be proved by you,
The evidence so great a proof doth carry.
But O see, see, we need inquire no further!
Upon your lips the scarlet drops are found,
And in your eye the boy that did the murder,
Your cheeks yet pale since first he gave the wound!
　　By this I see, however things be past,
　　Yet heaven will still have murder out at last.

III

Taking my pen, with words to cast my woe,
Duly to count the sum of all my cares,
I find my griefs innumerable grow,
The reck'nings rise to millions of despairs.
And thus dividing of my fatal hours,
The payments of my love I read and cross;
Subtracting, set my sweets unto my sours,
My joys' arrearage leads me to my loss.
And thus mine eyes a debtor to thine eye,
Which by extortion gaineth all their looks,
My heart hath paid such grievous usury,
That all their wealth lies in thy beauty's books.
    And all is thine which hath been due to me,
    And I a bankrupt, quite undone by thee.

IV

Bright star of beauty, on whose eyelids sit
A thousand nymph-like and enamoured graces,
The goddesses of memory and wit,
Which there in order take their several places;
In whose dear bosom, sweet delicious love
Lays down his quiver which he once did bear,
Since he that blessèd paradise did prove,
And leaves his mother's lap to sport him there
Let others strive to entertain with words
My soul is of a braver mettle made;
I hold that vile which vulgar wit affords;
In me's that faith which time cannot invade.
    Let what I praise be still made good by you;
    Be you most worthy whilst I am most true!

V

Nothing but 'No!' and 'I!' and 'I!' and 'No!'
'How falls it out so strangely?' you reply.
I tell ye, Fair, I'll not be answered so,
With this affirming 'No!' denying 'I!'
I say 'I love!' You slightly answer 'I!'
I say 'You love!' You pule me out a 'No!'
I say 'I die!' You echo me with 'I!'
'Save me!' I cry; you sigh me out a 'No!'
Must woe and I have naught but 'No!' and 'I!'?
No 'I!' am I, if I no more can have.
Answer no more; with silence make reply,
And let me take myself what I do crave;
    Let 'No!' and 'I!' with I and you be so,
      Then answer 'No!' and 'I!' and 'I!' and 'No!'

VI

How many paltry, foolish, painted things,
That now in coaches trouble every street,
Shall be forgotten, whom no poet sings,
Ere they be well wrapped in their winding sheet!
Where I to thee eternity shall give,
When nothing else remaineth of these days,
And queens hereafter shall be glad to live
Upon the alms of thy superfluous praise;
Virgins and matrons reading these my rhymes,
Shall be so much delighted with thy story,
That they shall grieve they lived not in these times,
To have seen thee, their sex's only glory.
    So shalt thou fly above the vulgar throng,
    Still to survive in my immortal song.

VII

Love, in a humour, played the prodigal,
And bade my senses to a solemn feast;
Yet more to grace the company withal,
Invites my heart to be the chiefest guest.
No other drink would serve this glutton's turn,
But precious tears distilling from mine eyne,
Which with my sighs this epicure doth burn,
Quaffing carouses in this costly wine;
Where, in his cups, o'ercome with foul excess,
Straightways he plays a swaggering ruffian's part,
And at the banquet in his drunkenness,
Slew his dear friend, my kind and truest heart.
    A gentle warning, friends, thus may you see,
    What 'tis to keep a drunkard company!

VIII

There's nothing grieves me but that age should haste,
That in my days I may not see thee old;
That where those two clear sparkling eyes are placed,
Only two loopholes that I might behold;
That lovely archèd ivory-polished brow
Defaced with wrinkles, that I might but see;
Thy dainty hair, so curled and crispèd now,
Like grizzled moss upon some agèd tree;
Thy cheek now flush with roses, sunk and lean;
Thy lips, with age as any wafer thin!
Thy pearly teeth out of thy head so clean,
That when thou feed'st thy nose shall touch thy chin!
    These lines that now thou scornst, which should
                     delight thee,
    Then would I make thee read but to despite thee.

IX

As other men, so I myself do muse
Why in this sort I wrest invention so,
And why these giddy metaphors I use,
Leaving the path the greater part do go.
I will resolve you. I'm a lunatic;
And ever this in madmen you shall find,
What they last thought of when the brain grew sick,
In most distraction they keep that in mind.
Thus talking idly in this bedlam fit,
Reason and I, you must conceive, are twain;
'Tis nine years now since first I lost my wit.
Bear with me then though troubled be my brain.
     With diet and correction men distraught,
     Not too far past, may to their wits be brought.

X

To nothing fitter can I thee compare
Than to the son of some rich penny-father,
Who having now brought on his end with care,
Leaves to his son all he had heaped together.
This new rich novice, lavish of his chest,
To one man gives, doth on another spend;
Then here he riots; yet amongst the rest,
Haps to lend some to one true honest friend.
Thy gifts thou in obscurity dost waste:
False friends, thy kindness born but to deceive thee;
Thy love that is on the unworthy placed;
Time hath thy beauty which with age will leave thee.
    Only that little which to me was lent,
    I give thee back when all the rest is spent.

XI

You're not alone when you are still alone;
O God! from you that I could private be!
Since you one were, I never since was one;
Since you in me, myself since out of me.
Transported from myself into your being,
Though either distant, present yet to either;
Senseless with too much joy, each other seeing;
And only absent when we are together.
Give me my self, and take your self again!
Devise some means but how I may forsake you!
So much is mine that doth with you remain,
That taking what is mine, with me I take you.
    You do bewitch me! O that I could fly
    From my self you, or from your own self I!

TO THE SOUL

XII

That learned Father which so firmly proves
The soul of man immortal and divine,
And doth the several offices define
Anima. Gives her that name, as she the body moves.
Amor. Then is she love, embracing charity.
Animus. Moving a will in us, it is the mind;
Mens. Retaining knowledge, still the same in kind.
Memoria. As intellectual, it is memory.
Ratio. In judging, reason only is her name.
Sensus. In speedy apprehension, it is sense.
Conscientia. In right and wrong they call her
                                    conscience;
Spiritus. The spirit, when it to God-ward doth inflame:
    These of the soul the several functions be,
    Which my heart lightened by thy love doth see.

TO THE SHADOW

XIII

Letters and lines we see are soon defaced
Metals do waste and fret with canker's rust,
The diamond shall once consume to dust,
And freshest colours with foul stains disgraced;
Paper and ink can paint but naked words,
To write with blood of force offends the sight;
And if with tears, I find them all too light,
And sighs and signs a silly hope affords.
O sweetest shadow, how thou serv'st my turn!
Which still shalt be as long as there is sun,
Nor whilst the world is never shall be done;
Whilst moon shall shine or any fire shall burn,
    That everything whence shadow doth proceed,
    May in his shadow my love's story read.

HIS REMEDY FOR LOVE

XV

Since to obtain thee nothing me will stead,
I have a med'cine that shall cure my love.
The powder of her heart dried, when she's dead,
That gold nor honour ne'er had power to move;
Mixed with her tears that ne'er her true love crost,
Nor at fifteen ne'er longed to be a bride;
Boiled with her sighs, in giving up the ghost,
That for her late deceasèd husband died;
Into the same then let a woman breathe,
That being chid did never word reply;
With one thrice married's prayers, that did bequeath
A legacy to stale virginity.
    If this receipt have not the power to win me,
    Little I'll say, but think the devil's in me!

AN ALLUSION TO THE PHŒNIX

XVI

'Mongst all the creatures in this spacious round
Of the birds' kind, the phœnix is alone,
Which best by you of living things is known;
None like to that, none like to you is found!
Your beauty is the hot and splend'rous sun;
The precious spices be your chaste desire,
Which being kindled by that heavenly fire,
Your life, so like the phœnix's begun.
Yourself thus burnèd in that sacred flame,
With so rare sweetness all the heavens perfuming;
Again increasing as you are consuming,
Only by dying born the very same.
  And winged by fame you to the stars ascend;
  So you of time shall live beyond the end.

TO TIME

XVII

Stay, speedy time! Behold, before thou pass
From age to age, what thou hast sought to see,
One in whom all the excellencies be,
In whom heaven looks itself as in a glass.
Time, look thou too in this translucent glass,
And thy youth past in this pure mirror see!
As the world's beauty in his infancy,
What it was then, and thou before it was.
Pass on and to posterity tell this—
Yet see thou tell but truly what hath been.
Say to our nephews that thou once hast seen
In perfect human shape all heavenly bliss;
 And bid them mourn, nay more, despair with thee,
 That she is gone, her like again to see.

TO THE CELESTIAL NUMBERS

XVIII

To this our world, to learning, and to heaven,
Three nines there are, to every one a nine;
One number of the earth, the other both divine;
One woman now makes three odd numbers even.
Nine orders first of angels be in heaven;
Nine muses do with learning still frequent:
These with the gods are ever resident.
Nine worthy women to the world were given.
My worthy one to these nine worthies addeth;
And my fair Muse, one Muse unto the nine.
And my good angel, in my soul divine!—
With one more order these nine orders gladdeth.
    My Muse, my worthy, and my angel then
    Makes every one of these three nines a ten.

TO HUMOUR

XIX

You cannot love, my pretty heart, and why?
There was a time you told me that you would,
But how again you will the same deny.
If it might please you, would to God you could!
What, will you hate? Nay, that you will not neither;
Nor love, nor hate! How then? What will you do?
What, will you keep a mean then betwixt either?
Or will you love me, and yet hate me too?
Yet serves not this! What next, what other shift?
You will, and will not; what a coil is here!
I see your craft, now I perceive your drift,
And all this while I was mistaken there.
    Your love and hate is this, I now do prove you:
    You love in hate, by hate to make me love you.

XX

An evil spirit, your beauty, haunts me still,
Wherewith, alas, I have been long possessed!
Which ceaseth not to tempt me to each ill,
Nor give me once but one poor minute's rest.
In me it speaks whether I sleep or wake;
And when by means to drive it out I try,
With greater torments then it me doth take,
And tortures me in most extremity.
Before my face it lays down my despairs,
And hastes me on unto a sudden death;
Now tempting me to drown myself in tears,
And then in sighing to give up my breath.
    Thus am I still provoked to every evil,
      By this good wicked spirit, sweet angel-devil.

XXI

A witless gallant a young wench that wooed—
Yet his dull spirit her not one jot could move—
Intreated me as e'er I wished his good,
To write him but one sonnet to his love.
When I as fast as e'er my pen could trot,
Poured out what first from quick invention came,
Nor never stood one word thereof to blot;
Much like his wit that was to use the same.
But with my verses he his mistress won,
Who doated on the dolt beyond all measure.
But see, for you to heaven for phrase I run,
And ransack all Apollo's golden treasure!
    Yet by my troth, this fool his love obtains,
    And I lose you for all my wit and pains!

TO FOLLY

XXII

With fools and children good discretion bears;
Then, honest people, bear with love and me,
Nor older yet nor wiser made by years,
Amongst the rest of fools and children be.
Love, still a baby, plays with gauds and toys,
And like a wanton sports with every feather,
And idiots still are running after boys;
Then fools and children fitt'st to go together.
He still as young as when he first was born,
Nor wiser I than when as young as he;
You that behold us, laugh us not to scorn;
Give nature thanks you are not such as we!
  Yet fools and children sometimes tell in play;
  Some wise in show, more fools indeed than they.

XXIII

Love, banished heaven, in earth was held in scorn,
Wand'ring abroad in need and beggary;
And wanting friends, though of a goddess born,
Yet craved the alms of such as passèd by.
I, like a man devout and charitable,
Clothèd the naked, lodged this wandering guest;
With sighs and tears still furnishing his table
With what might make the miserable blest.
But this ungrateful for my good desert,
Enticed my thoughts against me to conspire,
Who gave consent to steal away my heart,
And set my breast, his lodging, on a fire.
    Well, well, my friends, when beggars grow thus
                      bold,
    No marvel then though charity grow cold.

XXIV

I hear some say, 'This man is not in love!'
'Who! can he love? a likely thing!' they say.
'Read but his verse, and it will easily prove!'
O, judge not rashly, gentle Sir, I pray!
Because I loosely trifle in this sort,
As one that fain his sorrows would beguile,
You now suppose me all this time in sport,
And please yourself with this conceit the while.
Ye shallow cens'rers! sometimes, see ye not,
In greatest perils some men pleasant be,
Where fame by death is only to be got,
They resolute! So stands the case with me.
　　Where other men in depth of passion cry,
　　I laugh at fortune, as in jest to die.

XXV

O, why should nature niggardly restrain
That foreign nations relish not our tongue?
Else should my lines glide on the waves of Rhine,
And crown the Pyren's with my living song.
But bounded thus, to Scotland get you forth!
Thence take you wing unto the Orcades!
There let my verse get glory in the north,
Making my sighs to thaw the frozen seas.
And let the bards within that Irish isle,
To whom my Muse with fiery wings shall pass,
Call back the stiff-necked rebels from exile,
And mollify the slaughtering gallowglass;
    And when my flowing numbers they rehearse,
    Let wolves and bears be charmèd with my verse.

TO DESPAIR

XXVI

I ever love where never hope appears,
Yet hope draws on my never-hoping care,
And my life's hope would die but for despair;
My never certain joy breeds ever certain fears.
Uncertain dread gives wings unto my hope;
Yet my hope's wings are laden so with fear
As they cannot ascend to my hope's sphere,
Though fear gives them more than a heavenly scope.
Yet this large room is bounded with despair,
So my love is still fettered with vain hope,
And liberty deprives him of his scope,
And thus am I imprisoned in the air.
    Then, sweet despair, awhile hold up thy head,
    Or all my hope for sorrow will be dead.

XXVII

Is not love here as 'tis in other climes,
And differeth it as do the several nations?
Or hath it lost the virtue with the times,
Or in this island alt'reth with the fashions?
Or have our passions lesser power than theirs,
Who had less art them lively to express?
Is nature grown less powerful in their heirs,
Or in our fathers did she more transgress?
I am sure my sighs come from a heart as true
As any man's that memory can boast,
And my respects and services to you,
Equal with his that loves his mistress most.
    Or nature must be partial in my cause,
    Or only you do violate her laws.

XXVIII

To such as say thy love I overprize,
And do not stick to term my praises folly,
Against these folks that think themselves so wise,
I thus oppose my reason's forces wholly:
Though I give more than well affords my state,
In which expense the most suppose me vain
Which yields them nothing at the easiest rate,
Yet at this price returns me treble gain;
They value not, unskilful how to use,
And I give much because I gain thereby.
I that thus take or they that thus refuse,
Whether are these deceivèd then, or I?
    In everything I hold this maxim still,
      The circumstance doth make it good or ill.

TO THE SENSES

XXIX

When conquering love did first my heart assail,
Unto mine aid I summoned every sense,
Doubting if that proud tyrant should prevail,
My heart should suffer for mine eyes' offence.
But he with beauty first corrupted sight,
My hearing bribed with her tongue's harmony,
My taste by her sweet lips drawn with delight,
My smelling won with her breath's spicery,
But when my touching came to play his part,
The king of senses, greater than the rest,
He yields love up the keys unto my heart,
And tells the others how they should be blest.
    And thus by those of whom I hoped for aid,
    To cruel love my soul was first betrayed.

TO THE VESTALS

XXX

Those priests which first the vestal fire begun,
Which might be borrowed from no earthly flame,
Devised a vessel to receive the sun,
Being stedfastly opposèd to the same;
Where with sweet wood laid curiously by art,
On which the sun might by reflection beat,
Receiving strength for every secret part,
The fuel kindled with celestial heat.
Thy blessèd eyes, the sun which lights this fire,
My holy thoughts, they be the vestal flame,
Thy precious odours be my chaste desires,
My breast's the vessel which includes the same;
 Thou art my Vesta, thou my goddess art,
 Thy hallowed temple only is my heart.

TO THE CRITICS

XXXI

Methinks I see some crooked mimic jeer,
And tax my Muse with this fantastic grace;
Turning my papers asks, 'What have we here?'
Making withal some filthy antic face.
I fear no censure nor what thou canst say,
Nor shall my spirit one jot of vigour lose.
Think'st thou, my wit shall keep the packhorse way,
That every dudgeon low invention goes?
Since sonnets thus in bundles are imprest,
And every drudge doth dull our satiate ear,
Think'st thou my love shall in those rags be drest
That every dowdy, every trull doth wear?
    Up to my pitch no common judgment flies;
    I scorn all earthly dung-bred scarabies.

TO THE RIVER ANKOR

XXXII

Our floods' queen, Thames, for ships and swans is
crowned,
And stately Severn for her shore is praised;
The crystal Trent for fords and fish renowned,
And Avon's fame to Albion's cliff is raised.
Carlegion Chester vaunts her holy Dee;
York many wonders of her Ouse can tell;
The Peak, her Dove, whose banks so fertile be;
And Kent will say her Medway doth excel.
Cotswold commends her Isis to the Thame;
Our northern borders boast of Tweed's fair flood;
Our western parts extol their Wilis' fame;
And the old Lea brags of the Danish blood.
    Arden's sweet Ankor, let thy glory be,
    That fair Idea only lives by thee!

TO IMAGINATION

XXXIII

Whilst yet mine eyes do surfeit with delight,
My woful heart imprisoned in my breast,
Wisheth to be transformèd to my sight,
That it like those by looking might be blest.
But whilst mine eyes thus greedily do gaze,
Finding their objects over-soon depart,
These now the other's happiness do praise,
Wishing themselves that they had been my heart,
That eyes were heart, or that the heart were eyes,
As covetous the other's use to have.
But finding nature their request denies,
This to each other mutually they crave;
    That since the one cannot the other be,
    That eyes could think of that my heart could see.

TO ADMIRATION

XXXIV

Marvel not, love, though I thy power admire,
Ravished a world beyond the farthest thought,
And knowing more than ever hath been taught,
That I am only starved in my desire.
Marvel not, love, though I thy power admire,
Aiming at things exceeding all perfection,
To wisdom's self to minister direction,
That I am only starved in my desire.
Marvel not, love, though I thy power admire,
Though my conceit I further seem to bend
Than possibly invention can extend,
And yet am only starved in my desire.
    If thou wilt wonder, here's the wonder, love,
    That this to me doth yet no wonder prove.

TO MIRACLE

XXXV

Some misbelieving and profane in love,
When I do speak of miracles by thee,
May say that thou art flatterèd by me,
Who only write my skill in verse to prove
See miracles, ye unbelieving, see!
A dumb-born Muse made to express the mind,
A cripple hand to write, yet lame by kind,
One by thy name, the other touching thee.
Blind were mine eyes, till they were seen of thine;
And mine ears deaf by thy fame healèd be;
My vices cured by virtues sprung from thee;
My hopes revived which long in grave had lien.
    All unclean thoughts, foul spirits, cast out in me,
    Only by virtue that proceeds from thee.

CUPID CONJURED

XXXVI

Thou purblind boy, since thou hast been so slack
To wound her heart whose eyes have wounded me
And suffered her to glory in my wrack,
Thus to my aid I lastly conjure thee!
By hellish Styx, by which the Thund'rer swears,
By thy fair mother's unavoided power,
By Hecate's names, by Proserpine's sad tears,
When she was wrapt to the infernal bower!
By thine own lovèd Psyche, by the fires
Spent on thine altars flaming up to heaven,
By all true lovers' sighs, vows, and desires,
By all the wounds that ever thou hast given;
    I conjure thee by all that I have named,
      To make her love, or, Cupid, be thou damned!

XXXVII

Dear, why should you command me to my rest,
When now the night doth summon all to sleep?
Methinks this time becometh lovers best;
Night was ordained together friends to keep.
How happy are all other living things,
Which though the day disjoin by several flight,
The quiet evening yet together brings,
And each returns unto his love at night!
O thou that art so courteous else to all,
Why shouldst thou, Night, abuse me only thus,
That every creature to his kind dost call,
And yet 'tis thou dost only sever us?
    Well could I wish it would be ever day,
    If when night comes, you bid me go away.

XXXVIII

Sitting alone, love bids me go and write;
Reason plucks back, commanding me to stay,
Boasting that she doth still direct the way,
Or else love were unable to indite.
Love growing angry, vexèd at the spleen,
And scorning reason's maimèd argument,
Straight taxeth reason, wanting to invent
Where she with love conversing hath not been.
Reason reproachèd with this coy disdain,
Despiteth love, and laugheth at her folly;
And love contemning reason's reason wholly,
Thought it in weight too light by many a grain.
    Reason put back doth out of sight remove,
    And love alone picks reason out of love.

XXXIX

Some, when in rhyme they of their loves do tell,
With flames and lightnings their exordiums paint.
Some call on heaven, some invocate on hell,
And Fates and Furies, with their woes acquaint.
Elizium is too high a seat for me,
I will not come in Styx or Phlegethon,
The thrice-three Muses but too wanton be,
Like they that lust, I care not, I will none.
Spiteful Erinnys frights me with her looks,
My manhood dares not with foul Ate mell,
I quake to look on Hecate's charming books,
I still fear bugbears in Apollo's cell.
    I pass not for Minerva, nor Astrea,
    Only I call on my divine Idea!

XL

My heart the anvil where my thoughts do beat,
My words the hammers fashioning my desire,
My breast the forge including all the heat,
Love is the fuel which maintains the fire;
My sighs the bellows which the flame increaseth,
Filling mine ears with noise and nightly groaning;
Toiling with pain, my labour never ceaseth,
In grievous passions my woes still bemoaning;
My eyes with tears against the fire striving,
Whose scorching gleed my heart to cinders turneth;
But with those drops the flame again reviving,
Still more and more it to my torment burneth,
    With Sisyphus thus do I roll the stone,
    And turn the wheel with damnèd Ixion.

LOVE'S LUNACY

XLI

Why do I speak of joy or write of love,
When my heart is the very den of horror,
And in my soul the pains of hell I prove,
With all his torments and infernal terror?
What should I say? what yet remains to do?
My brain is dry with weeping all too long;
My sighs be spent in utt'ring of my woe,
And I want words wherewith to tell my wrong.
But still distracted in love's lunacy,
And bedlam-like thus raving in my grief,
Now rail upon her hair, then on her eye,
Now call her goddess, then I call her thief;
    Now I deny her, then I do confess her,
    Now do I curse her, then again I bless her.

XLII

Some men there be which like my method well,
And much commend the strangeness of my vein;
Some say I have a passing pleasing strain,
Some say that in my humour I excel.
Some who not kindly relish my conceit,
They say, as poets do, I use to feign,
And in bare words paint out by passions' pain.
Thus sundry men their sundry minds repeat.
I pass not, I, how men affected be,
Nor who commends or discommends my verse!
It pleaseth me if I my woes rehearse,
And in my lines if she my love may see.
    Only my comfort still consists in this,
    Writing her praise I cannot write amiss.

XLIII

Why should your fair eyes with such sov'reign grace
Disperse their rays on every vulgar spirit,
Whilst I in darkness in the self-same place,
Get not one glance to recompense my merit?
So doth the plowman gaze the wand'ring star,
And only rest contented with the light,
That never learned what constellations are,
Beyond the bent of his unknowing sight.
O why should beauty, custom to obey,
To their gross sense apply herself so ill!
Would God I were as ignorant as they,
When I am made unhappy by my skill,
    Only compelled on this poor good to boast!
    Heavens are not kind to them that know them most.

XLIV

Whilst thus my pen strives to eternise thee,
Age rules my lines with wrinkles in my face,
Where in the map of all my misery
Is modelled out the world of my disgrace;
Whilst in despite of tyrannising times,
Medea-like, I make thee young again,
Proudly thou scorn'st my world-outwearing rhymes,
And murther'st virtue with thy coy disdain;
And though in youth my youth untimely perish,
To keep thee from oblivion and the grave,
Ensuing ages yet my rhymes shall cherish,
Where I intombed my better part shall save;
    And though this earthly body fade and die,
    My name shall mount upon eternity.

XLV

Muses which sadly sit about my chair,
Drowned in the tears extorted by my lines;
With heavy sighs whilst thus I break the air,
Painting my passions in these sad designs,
Since she disdains to bless my happy verse,
The strong built trophies to her living fame,
Ever henceforth my bosom be your hearse,
Wherein the world shall now entomb her name.
Enclose my music, you poor senseless walls,
Sith she is deaf and will not hear my moans;
Soften yourselves with every tear that falls,
Whilst I like Orpheus sing to trees and stones,
     Which with my plaint seem yet with pity moved,
     Kinder than she whom I so long have loved.

XLVI

Plain-pathed experience, the unlearnèd's guide,
Her simple followers evidently shows
Sometimes what schoolmen scarcely can decide,
Nor yet wise reason absolutely knows;
In making trial of a murder wrought,
If the vile actors of the heinous deed
Near the dead body happily be brought,
Oft 't hath been proved the breathless corse will bleed.
She coming near, that my poor heart hath slain,
Long since departed, to the world no more,
The ancient wounds no longer can contain,
But fall to bleeding as they did before.
    But what of this? Should she to death be led,
    It furthers justice but helps not the dead.

XLVII

In pride of wit, when high desire of fame
Gave life and courage to my lab'ring pen,
And first the sound and virtue of my name
Won grace and credit in the ears of men,
With those the throngèd theatres that press,
I in the circuit for the laurel strove,
Where the full praise I freely must confess,
In heat of blood a modest mind might move;
With shouts and claps at every little pause,
When the proud round on every side hath rung,
Sadly I sit unmoved with the applause,
As though to me it nothing did belong.
    No public glory vainly I pursue;
    All that I seek is to eternise you.

XLVIII

Cupid, I hate thee, which I'd have thee know;
A naked starveling ever mayst thou be!
Poor rogue, go pawn thy fascia and thy bow
For some poor rags wherewith to cover thee;
Or if thou'lt not thy archery forbear,
To some base rustic do thyself prefer,
And when corn's sown or grown into the ear,
Practice thy quiver and turn crowkeeper;
Or being blind, as fittest for the trade,
Go hire thyself some bungling harper's boy;
They that are blind are minstrels often made,
So mayst thou live to thy fair mother's joy;
  That whilst with Mars she holdeth her old way,
  Thou, her blind son, mayst sit by them and play.

XLIX

Thou leaden brain, which censur'st what I write,
And sayst my lines be dull and do not move,
I marvel not thou feel'st not my delight,
Which never felt'st my fiery touch of love;
But thou whose pen hath like a packhorse served,
Whose stomach unto gall hath turned thy food,
Whose senses like poor prisoners, hunger-starved
Whose grief hath parched thy body, dried thy blood;
Thou which hast scornèd life and hated death,
And in a moment, mad, sober, glad, and sorry;
Thou which hast banned thy thoughts and curst thy birth
With thousand plagues more than in purgatory;
 Thou thus whose spirit love in his fire refines,
 Come thou and read, admire, applaud my lines!

L

As in some countries far remote from hence,
The wretched creature destinèd to die,
Having the judgment due to his offence,
By surgeons begged, their art on him to try,
Which on the living work without remorse,
First make incision on each mastering vein,
Then staunch the bleeding, then transpierce the corse,
And with their balms recure the wounds again,
Then poison and with physic him restore;
Not that they fear the hopeless man to kill,
But their experience to increase the more:
Even so my mistress works upon my ill,
  By curing me and killing me each hour,
  Only to show her beauty's sovereign power.

LI

Calling to mind since first my love begun,
Th'uncertain times, oft varying in their course,
How things still unexpectedly have run,
As't please the Fates by their resistless force;
Lastly, mine eyes amazedly have seen
Essex's great fall, Tyrone his peace to gain,
The quiet end of that long living Queen,
This King's fair entrance, and our peace with Spain,
We and the Dutch at length ourselves to sever;
Thus the world doth and evermore shall reel;
Yet to my goddess am I constant ever,
Howe'er blind Fortune turn her giddy wheel;
  Though heaven and earth prove both to me untrue,
  Yet am I still inviolate to you.

LII

What dost thou mean to cheat me of my heart,
To take all mine and give me none again?
Or have thine eyes such magic or that art
That what they get they ever do retain?
Play not the tyrant but take some remorse;
Rebate thy spleen if but for pity's sake;
Or cruel, if thou can'st not, let us scorse,
And for one piece of thine my whole heart take.
But what of pity do I speak to thee,
Whose breast is proof against complaint or prayer?
Or can I think what my reward shall be
From that proud beauty which was my betrayer!
    What talk I of a heart when thou hast none?
    Or if thou hast, it is a flinty one.

ANOTHER TO THE RIVER ANKOR

LIII

Clear Ankor, on whose silver-sanded shore,
My soul-shrined saint, my fair Idea lives;
O blessèd brook, whose milk-white swans adore
Thy crystal stream, refinèd by her eyes,
Where sweet myrrh-breathing Zephyr in the spring
Gently distils his nectar-dropping showers,
Where nightingales in Arden sit and sing
Amongst the dainty dew-impearlèd flowers;
Say thus, fair brook, when thou shalt see thy queen,
'Lo, here thy shepherd spent his wand'ring years
And in these shades, dear nymph, he oft hath been;
And here to thee he sacrificed his tears.'
   Fair Arden, thou my Tempe art alone,
   And thou, sweet Ankor, art my Helicon!

LIV

Yet read at last the story of my woe,
The dreary abstracts of my endless cares,
With my life's sorrow interlinèd so,
Smoked with my sighs, and blotted with my tears,
The sad memorials of my miseries,
Penned in the grief of mine afflicted ghost,
My life's complaint in doleful elegies,
With so pure love as time could never boast.
Receive the incense which I offer here,
By my strong faith ascending to thy fame,
My zeal, my hope, my vows, my praise, my prayer,
My soul's oblations to thy sacred name;
 Which name my Muse to highest heavens shall raise,
 By chaste desire, true love, and virtuous praise.

LV

My fair, if thou wilt register my love,
A world of volumes shall thereof arise;
Preserve my tears, and thou thyself shall prove
A second flood down raining from mine eyes;
Note but my sighs, and thine eyes shall behold
The sunbeams smothered with immortal smoke;
And if by thee my prayers may be enrolled,
They heaven and earth to pity shall provoke.
Look thou into my breast, and thou shalt see
Chaste holy vows for my soul's sacrifice,
That soul, sweet maid, which so hath honoured thee,
Erecting trophies to thy sacred eyes,
    Those eyes to my heart shining ever bright,
    When darkness hath obscured each other light.

AN ALLUSION TO THE EAGLETS

LVI

When like an eaglet I first found my love,
For that the virtue I thereof would know,
Upon the nest I set it forth to prove
If it were of that kingly kind or no;
But it no sooner saw my sun appear,
But on her rays with open eyes it stood,
To show that I had hatched it for the air,
And rightly came from that brave mounting brood;
And when the plumes were summed with sweet desire,
To prove the pinions it ascends the skies;
Do what I could, it needsly would aspire
To my soul's sun, those two celestial eyes.
    Thus from my breast, where it was bred alone,
    It after thee is like an eaglet flown.

LVII

You best discerned of my mind's inward eyes,
And yet your graces outwardly divine,
Whose dear remembrance in my bosom lies,
Too rich a relic for so poor a shrine;
You, in whom nature chose herself to view,
When she her own perfection would admire;
Bestowing all her excellence on you,
At whose pure eyes Love lights his hallowed fire;
Even as a man that in some trance hath seen
More than his wond'ring utterance can unfold,
That rapt in spirit in better worlds hath been,
So must your praise distractedly be told;
    Most of all short when I would show you most,
    In your perfections so much am I lost.

LVIII

In former times, such as had store of coin,
In wars at home or when for conquests bound,
For fear that some their treasure should purloin,
Gave it to keep to spirits within the ground;
And to attend it them as strongly tied
Till they returned. Home when they never came,
Such as by art to get the same have tried,
From the strong spirit by no means force the same.
Nearer men come, that further flies away,
Striving to hold it strongly in the deep.
Ev'n as this spirit, so you alone do play
With those rich beauties Heav'n gives you to keep;
    Pity so left to th' coldness of your blood,
    Not to avail you nor do others good.

TO PROVERBS

As Love and I late harboured in one inn,
With Proverbs thus each other entertain.
'In love there is no lack,' thus I begin:
'Fair words make fools,' replieth he again.
'Who spares to speak, doth spare to speed,' quoth I.
'As well,' saith he, 'too forward as too slow.'
'Fortune assists the boldest,' I reply.
'A hasty man,' quoth he, 'ne'er wanted woe!'
'Labour is light, where love,' quoth I, 'doth pay.'
Saith he, 'Light burden's heavy, if far born.'
Quoth I, 'The main lost, cast the by away!'
'You have spun a fair thread,' he replies in scorn.
   And having thus awhile each other thwarted,
   Fools as we met, so fools again we parted.

LX

Define my weal, and tell the joys of heaven;
Express my woes and show the pains of hell;
Declare what fate unlucky stars have given,
And ask a world upon my life to dwell;
Make known the faith that fortune could no move,
Compare my worth with others' base desert,
Let virtue be the touchstone of my love,
So may the heavens read wonders in my heart;
Behold the clouds which have eclipsed my sun,
And view the crosses which my course do let;
Tell me, if ever since the world begun
So fair a rising had so foul a set?
    And see if time, if he would strive to prove,
    Can show a second to so pure a love.

LXI

Since there's no help, come let us kiss and part,
Nay I have done, you get no more of me;
And I am glad, yea glad with all my heart,
That thus so cleanly I myself can free;
Shakes hands for ever, cancel all our vows,
And when we meet at any time again,
Be it not seen in either of our brows
That we one jot of former love retain.
Now at the last gasp of Love's latest breath,
When his pulse failing, Passion speechless lies,
When Faith is kneeling by his bed of death,
And Innocence is closing up his eyes:
 Now if thou wouldst, when all have given him over,
 From death to life thou might'st him yet recover!

圖 73

LXII

When first I ended, then I first began;
Then more I travelled further from my rest.
Where most I lost, there most of all I won;
Pinèd with hunger, rising from a feast.
Methinks I fly, yet want I legs to go,
Wise in conceit, in act a very sot,
Ravished with joy amidst a hell of woe,
What most I seem that surest am I not.
I build my hopes a world above the sky,
Yet with the mole I creep into the earth;
In plenty I am starved with penury,
And yet I surfeit in the greatest dearth.
    I have, I want, despair, and yet desire,
      Burned in a sea of ice, and drowned amidst a fire.

LXIII

Truce, gentle Love, a parley now I crave,
Methinks 'tis long since first these wars begun;
Nor thou, nor I, the better yet can have;
Bad is the match where neither party won.
I offer free conditions of fair peace,
My heart for hostage that it shall remain.
Discharge our forces, here let malice cease,
So for my pledge thou give me pledge again.
Or if no thing but death will serve thy turn,
Still thirsting for subversion of my state,
Do what thou canst, raze, massacre, and burn;
Let the world see the utmost of thy hate;
    I send defiance, since if overthrown,
    Thou vanquishing, the conquest is mine own.

A NOTE ON MICHAEL DRAYTON

Michael Drayton was born in 1563 in Warwickshire. He worked as a page (for Sir Henry Goodyere, an early patron, and later for Lucy, Countess of Bedford), and esquire (for Sir Walter Aston). As well as poems he wrote plays (1597-1602). He died in 1631 and is buried in Westminster Abbey.

Michael Drayton's *Idea In Sixtie Three Sonnets* was revised a number of times by the author. It was published first in 1594, and was republished in 1599, 1600, 1602, 1605 and 1619. Anne Goodyere (the daughter of Sir Philip Sidney's friend Sir Henry Goodyere) is assumed to be the object of affection in the sonnet sequence (though it's not certain if they were romantically involved; Drayton remained a passionate admirer for most of his life, and hers. She was married to Sir Henry Rainsford from 1595 until Rainsford's death in 1622, after which Drayton continued as Anne's devotee). The name *Idea* also has Platonic associations.

The text is from *Elizabethan Sonnet Cycles,* edited by Martha Foote Crow, Kegan Paul, Trench, Trübner & Co., London, 1897.

FURTHER READING

MICHAEL DRAYTON

The Works of Michael Drayton, ed. J. Hebel, Oxford, 1931-41
Poems, Scolar Press, 1969
Poems of Michael Drayton, ed. J. Buxton, London, 1963

HIGHLY RECOMMENDED

The following books are excellent introductions to the
Elizabethan sonnet. Maurice Evans' *Elizabethan Sonnets* (1977,
later revised, in 1994) is one of the best books as an all-round
collection of Elizabethan sonneteering.

Maurice Evans, ed. *Elizabethan Sonnets*, Dent, 1977/ 94
G. Hiller, ed. *Poems of the Elizabethan Age*, Methuen, 1977
E. Lucie-Smith, ed. *The Penguin Book of Elizabethan Verse*,
    Penguin, 1965
Michael R.G. Spiller. *The Development of the Sonnet: An Intro-
    duction*, Routledge, 1992
Maurice Valency. *In Praise of Love: An Introduction to the Love-
    Poetry of the Renaissance*, Macmillan, New York, 1961

OTHER BOOKS

Books marked with an asterisk are especially useful.

Sandra Berman. *The Sonnet Over Time*, Chapel Hill, 1988 •

Harold Bloom, ed. *Shakespeare's Sonnets* Chelsea House, New York, 1987

—. *Hamlet*, Chelsea House, New York, 1990

S. Booth. *An Essay on Shakespeare's Sonnets* Yale University Press, 1969

S.C. Campbell. *Only Begotten Sonnets: A Reconstruction of Shakespeare's Sonnets Sequence* Bell & Hyman, 1978

Reed Way Dasenbrock. *Imitating the Italians: Wyatt, Spenser, Syne, Pound, Joyce,* John Hopkins University Press, Baltimore, 1991

Heather Dubrow. *Captive Victors: Shakespeare's Narrative Poems and Sonnets*, Cornell University Press, Ithaca, 1987

—. *Echoes of Desire: English Petrarchism and Its Counter-discourses,* Cornell University Press, 1995 *

Joel Fineman. *Shakespeare's Perjured Eye: The Invention of Poetic Subjectivity in the Sonnets* University of California Press, 1988*

Edward Hubler. *The Sense of Shakespeare's Sonnets* Hill & Wang, New York, 1962

J.B. Leishman. *Themes and Variations in Shakespeare's Sonnets* Hillary House, New York, 1963

J. W. Lever. *The Elizabethan Love Sonnet* Methuen, 1956

Arthur Marotti. ""Love is not love": Elizabethan Sonnet Sequences and the Social Order", *English Literary History,* 49, 1982

Kenneth Muir. *Shakespeare's Sonnets* Allen & Unwin, 1979

G.M. Ridden. *Shakespeare's Sonnets* Longman, 1982

Brent Stirling. *The Shakespeare Sonnet Order: Poems and Groups* University of California Press, Berkeley, 1968

J.C. Wait. *The Background to Shakespeare's Sonnets* Chatto & Windus, 1972

James Winny. *The Master-Mistress: A Study of Shakespeare's Sonnets*, Chatto & Windus, 1968

In the Dim Void

Samuel Beckett's Late Trilogy:
Company, Ill Seen, Ill Said and *Worstward Ho*

by Gregory Johns

This book discusses the luminous beauty and dense, rigorous poetry of Samuel Beckett's late works, *Company, Ill Seen, Ill Said* and *Worstward Ho*. Gregory Johns looks back over Beckett's long writing career, charting the development from the *Molloy-Malone Dies-Unnamable* trilogy through the 'fizzles' of the 1960s to the elegiac lyricism of the *Company* series. Johns compares the trilogy with late plays such as *Ghosts, Footfalls* and *Rockaby*.

Bibliography, notes. Illustrated. 120pp
ISBN 9781861712974 Pbk and ISBN 9781861712608 Hbk
9781861713407 E-book

Beauties, Beasts, and Enchantment

CLASSIC FRENCH FAIRY TALES

Translated and with an Introduction
by Jack Zipes

A collection of 36 classic French fairy tales translated by renowned writer Jack Zipes. *Cinderella, Beauty and the Beast, Sleeping Beauty* and *Little Red Riding Hood* are among the classic fairy tales in this amazing book.
Includes illustrations from fairy tale collections.
Jack Zipes has written and published widely on fairy tales.

'Terrific... a succulent array of 17th and 18th century 'salon' fairy tales'
- *The New York Times Book Review*
'Enjoyable to read... a unique collection of French regional folklore' - *Library Journal*
'Charming stories accompanied by attractive pen-and-ink drawings' - *Chattanooga Times*

Introduction and illustrations 612pp.   ISBN 9781861712510 Pbk   ISBN 9781861713193 Hbk

MAURICE SENDAK

& the art of children's book illustration

L.M. Poole

Maurice Sendak is the widely acclaimed American children's book author and illustrator. This critical study focuses on his famous trilogy, *Where the Wild Things Are, In the Night Kitchen* and *Outside Over There,* as well as the early works and Sendak's superb depictions of the Grimm Brothers' fairy tales in *The Juniper Tree.* L.M. Poole begins with a chapter on children's book illustration, in particular the treatment of fairy tales. Sendak's work is situated within the history of children's book illustration, and he is compared with many contemporary authors.

Fully illustrated. The book has been revised and updated for this edition.
ISBN 9781861714282 Pbk   ISBN 9781861713469 Hbk

ARTS, PAINTING, SCULPTURE

web: www.crmoon.com • e-mail: cresmopub@yahoo.co.uk

The Art of Andy Goldsworthy
Andy Goldsworthy: Touching Nature
Andy Goldsworthy in Close-Up
Andy Goldsworthy: Pocket Guide
Andy Goldsworthy In America

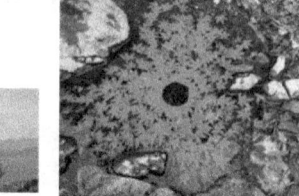

Land Art: A Complete Guide
The Art of Richard Long
Richard Long: Pocket Guide
Land Art In Great Britain
Land Art in Close-Up
Land Art In the U.S.A.
Land Art: Pocket Guide
Installation Art in Close-Up

Minimal Art and Artists In the 1960s and After
Colourfield Painting
Land Art DVD, TV documentary
Andy Goldsworthy DVD, TV documentary
The Erotic Object: Sexuality in Sculpture From Prehistory to the Present Day
Sex in Art: Pornography and Pleasure in Painting and Sculpture
Postwar Art
Sacred Gardens: The Garden in Myth, Religion and Art
Glorification: Religious Abstraction in Renaissance and 20th Century Art
Early Netherlandish Painting
Jasper Johns
Brice MardenLeonardo da Vinci
Piero della Francesca
Giovanni Bellini

Fra Angelico: Art and Religion in the Renaissance
Mark Rothko: The Art of Transcendence
Frank Stella: American Abstract Artist
Alison Wilding: The Embrace of Sculpture
Vincent van Gogh: Visionary Landscapes
Eric Gill: Nuptials of God
Constantin Brancusi: Sculpting the Essence of Things
Max Beckmann
Gustave Moreau
Caravaggio

Egon Schiele: Sex and Death In Purple Stockings
Delizioso Fotografico Fervore: Works In Process I
Sacro Cuore: Works In Process 2
The Light Eternal: J.M.W. Turner
The Madonna Glorified: Karen Arthurs

LITERATURE

J.R.R. Tolkien: The Books, The Films, The Whole Cultural Phenomenon
J.R.R. Tolkien: Pocket Guide
Beauties, Beasts and Enchantment: Classic French Fairy Tales
Tolkien's Heroic Quest

Brothers Grimm: German Popular Stories
Sexing Hardy: Thomas Hardy and Feminism
Thomas Hardy's *Tess of the d'Urbervilles*
Thomas Hardy's *Jude the Obscure*
Thomas Hardy: The Tragic Novels
Love and Tragedy: Thomas Hardy
The Poetry of Landscape in Hardy
Wessex Revisited: Thomas Hardy and John Cowper Powys

Wolfgang Iser: Essays and Interviews
Petrarch, Dante and the Troubadours
Maurice Sendak and the Art of Children's Book Illustration
Andrea Dworkin
Cixous, Irigaray, Kristeva: The *Jouissance* of French Feminism
Julia Kristeva: Art, Love, Melancholy, Philosophy, Semiotics and Psychoanalysis
Hélene Cixous I Love You: The *Jouissance* of Writing
Luce Irigaray: Lips, Kissing, and the Politics of Sexual Difference
Peter Redgrove: Here Comes the Flood
Peter Redgrove: Sex-Magic-Poetry-Cornwall

Lawrence Durrell: Between Love and Death, East and West
Love, Culture & Poetry: Lawrence Durrell
Cavafy: Anatomy of a Soul
German Romantic Poetry: Goethe, Novalis, Heine, Hölderlin
Novalis: *Hymns To the Night*
Feminism and Shakespeare
Shakespeare: *The Sonnets*
Shakespeare: Love, Poetry & Magic
The Passion of D.H. Lawrence
D.H. Lawrence: Symbolic Landscapes
D.H. Lawrence: Infinite Sensual Violence
The Ecstasies of John Cowper Powys
Sensualism and Mythology: The Wessex Novels of John Cowper Powys
Amorous Life: John Cowper Powys (H.W. Fawkner)
Postmodern Powys: New Essays on John Cowper Powys (Joe Boulter)
Rethinking Powys: Critical Essays on John Cowper Powys
Paul Bowles & Bernardo Bertolucci
Rainer Maria Rilke
Joseph Conrad: *Heart of Darkness*

In the Dim Void: Samuel Beckett
Samuel Beckett Goes into the Silence
André Gide: Fiction and Fervour

Jackie Collins and the Blockbuster Novel
Blinded By Her Light: The Love-Poetry of Robert Graves

POETRY

Ursula Le Guin: *Walking In Cornwall*
Peter Redgrove: Here Comes The Flood
Peter Redgrove: Sex-Magic-Poetry-Cornwall
Dante: Selections From the *Vita Nuova*
Petrarch, Dante and the Troubadours
William Shakespeare: *The Sonnets*
William Shakespeare: Complete Poems
Blinded By Her Light: The Love-Poetry of Robert Graves
Emily Dickinson: Selected Poems
Emily Brontë: Poems

Thomas Hardy: Selected Poems
Percy Bysshe Shelley: Poems
John Keats: Selected Poems
John Keats: Poems of 1820
D.H. Lawrence: Selected Poems
Edmund Spenser: Poems
Edmund Spenser: *Amoretti*
John Donne: Poems
Henry Vaughan: Poems
Sir Thomas Wyatt: Poems

Robert Herrick: Selected Poems
Rilke: Space, Essence and Angels in the Poetry of Rainer Maria Rilke
Rainer Maria Rilke: Selected Poems
Friedrich Hölderlin: Selected Poems
Arseny Tarkovsky: Selected Poems
Paul Verlaine: Selected Poems

Novalis: *Hymns To the Night*
Arthur Rimbaud: Selected Poems
Arthur Rimbaud: *A Season in Hell*
Arthur Rimbaud and the Magic of Poetry
D.J. Enright: By-Blows
Jeremy Reed: *Brigitte's Blue Heart*
Jeremy Reed: *Claudia Schiffer's Red Shoes*
Gorgeous Little Orpheus
Radiance: New Poems
Crescent Moon Book of Nature Poetry

Crescent Moon Book of Love Poetry
Crescent Moon Book of Mystical Poetry
Crescent Moon Book of Elizabethan Love Poetry
Crescent Moon Book of Metaphysical Poetry
Crescent Moon Book of Romantic Poetry
Pagan America: New American Poetry

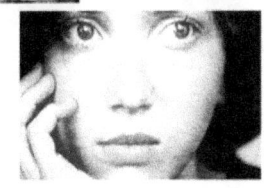

www.ingramcontent.com/pod-product-compliance
Lightning Source LLC
Chambersburg PA
CBHW072039170626
46811CB00008B/3108